MORE SUNDAY PUZZLES

MORE SUNDAY PUZZLES

by

Cyril Barnes

Drawings by
JAMES MOSS

HODDER AND STOUGHTON
LONDON SYDNEY AUCKLAND TORONTO

British Library Cataloguing in Publication data
Barnes, Cyril
    More Sunday Puzzles.
    1. Crossword puzzles
    2. Bible games and puzzles
    I. Title
    793.73'2   GV1507.C7

ISBN 0-340-24732-0

First published 1979.

Printed in Great Britain for
Hodder and Stoughton Ltd.,
Mill Road, Dunton Green, Sevenoaks, Kent
by Cox & Wyman Ltd., Reading.

Throughout the book the Authorized Version of the Bible (King James) is used for spelling and variation of words

Puzzles

1. It's in the Bible

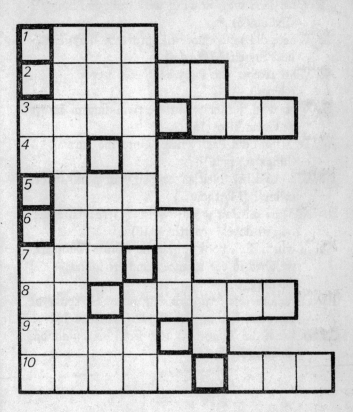

MANY expressions from the Bible have come into everyday use in English. Write the answers to the following questions in the squares provided and you will find that the letters in the thickened squares, read downwards, give the answer to the extra question

1. Over whom was David lamenting when he said: 'Tell it not in Gath'? (2 Samuel 1)

2. What land was 'flowing with milk and honey'? (Exodus 3)

3. Where did Jesus quote the proverb, 'Physician, heal thyself'? (Luke 4)

4. Who asked, 'Am I my brother's keeper'? (Genesis 4)

5. Who used the term, 'In the twinkling of an eye'? (1 Corinthians 15)

6. To whom did Paul write, 'Unto the pure all things are pure'?

7. Who told us, 'Neither cast ye your pearls before swine'? (Matthew 7)

8. Add the missing word: 'Wise as serpents, and . . . as doves' (Matthew 10)

9. In which Bible book appear the words: 'Thou art weighed in the balances, and art found wanting'?

10. Of whom was Jesus thinking when He spoke of the blind leading the blind? (Matthew 15)

Extra. What did Timothy know from his childhood? (2 Timothy 3)

2. Crossword

ACROSS

1. Devil
3. Bishop's area
5. Short for Edward
6. Prefix meaning 'one'
7. French for 'the'
9. Lot fled to this city (Genesis 19)
11. Grave
13. Old English money

11

14. Bird of prey
15. Mineral
16. Also
17. Disciples plucked these on the Sabbath day
     (Matthew 12)
20. Prophetess daughter of Phanuel (Luke 2)
22. Sounds like a girl's name
23. Vase
24. Morning
25. An age
26. Droop

DOWN

1. Language like
    Esperanto
2. Money bag
3. Keep one's seat
4. Tree
5. Prophet
8. Patriarch
10. Place of sacrifice
12. Group of stars
15. Cries
18. Champion airman
19. Source of light
21. Find fault

3. Miracles and wonders

UNJUMBLE the capital letters at the end of each sentence to give the right name.

A. In the Gospels

1. Tribute money was found in a fish's mouth in MACAPRUNE . . . .

2. Jesus quietened a storm on the Sea of ELILAGE . . . .

3. A blind man was healed in the pool of MAILOS . . . .

4. Jesus brought Lazarus back to life at TYBAHEN . . . .

5. A widow's son was restored to life at ANNI . . . .

6. Bartimaeus was made to\see near CHROJIE . . . .

7. Jesus escaped from an angry crowd at THAZERAN . . . .

8. A man with an unclean spirit was healed in the country of the NEADRAGES . . . .

9. A blind man was healed at SHEADABIT . . . .

B. In the Old Testament

1. Naaman was cured of leprosy in the river DROJAN . . . .
2. Moses made bitter waters sweet at AHARM
   . . . .
3. A widow's cooking oil and meal lasted as long as her need at THREAPHAZ
   . . . .
4. Moses made water come out of a rock while the Children of Israel were at PRIMEHID
   . . . .
5. In Joshua's day the moon stood still in the valley of JOANAL
6. Moses' rod turned into a serpent in front of RHOPAHA . . . .
7. Elijah's sacrifice was burned by 'the fire of the Lord' on LACMER . . . .
8. Daniel was unharmed by lions when thrown into a den by IDUSAR . . . .
9. God preserved Jonah inside a great fish when he failed to go to HENVINE . . . .

4. Squared off

THE main words fill the 7, 8, 9, 10, 11, 12 and 13 squares and can be built up by answering the three or four clues for each puzzle, placing the letters in the squares according to their number.

A.

1	2	3	4	5	6	7

Main word (1–7): Paul took this when he met the brethren on the road to Rome.
5, 1, 7: great flyer; 6, 2: proceed; 3, 4: birthplace of Abraham

B.

1	2	3	4	5	6	7	8

Main word (1–8): omnipotent.
3, 8: belonging to me; 6, 4, 7: tap; 2, 1, 5: fall behind

C.

1	2	3	4	5	6	7	8	9

Main word (1–9): witness.
3, 4, 9: pig's home; 6, 5, 8, 2: where coal or gold comes from;
1, 7: . . . and fro

D.

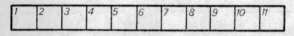

Main word (1–10): Book of the Bible.
5, 8, 3, 4: exist; 7, 2, 6: beverage; 10, 9, 1: neither

E.

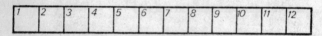

Main word (1–11): one who grossly overcharges.
3, 10, 2, 6: verse of Scripture; 11, 7, 4: . . . de
Janiero;
9, 1, 5, 8: Roman Emperor

F.

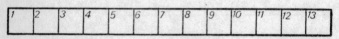

Main word (1–12): prayer for others.
8, 1, 3: not stand; 5, 10, 12, 9, 4: cleanse;
6, 11, 2, 7: fruit of a pine tree

G.

Main word (1–13): God treats pardoned sin with this.
4, 11, 10, 6: man; 2, 7: belonging to;
9, 5, 12, 13: fewer than; 1, 8, 3: animal's coat

16

5. Crossword

1. Negative
4. Strike
7. He tried to walk on the water to Jesus
9. So be it
11. Planet
13. A lion's whelp (Deuteronomy 33)
15. Another spelling for Noah
16. Type of music
18. Indefinite article
19. Joshua's men viewed this place (Joshua 7)
21. Epistle
25. Translated by faith (Hebrews 11)
26. Enemy
27. It must be inclined (Isaiah 55)

DOWN

2. Not closed
3. Half a score
4. Border
5. Persia
6. Insane
8. A vessel meet for the master's . . . (2 Timothy 2)
10. Food in the wilderness
12. Empire of Bible times
14. Negative
16. Smoothing tool
17. Cost
18. Length of life
20. Ending of many words
22. Lion
23. In the direction of
24. Expression of surprise

6. Filling the gap

FILL in the missing words in capital letters and you will find that these words read downwards will give you a well-known verse from the Bible:

A.
1. . . . . Lord is my shepherd
2. Innocent of the . . . . of this just person
3. I am the light . . . . the world
4. Thou shall call his name . . . .
5. Thou art the . . . . the Son of God
6. The Lord knoweth them that are . . . .
7. This is my beloved . . . . in whom I am well pleased
8. Heal the sick . . . . (th)the lepers, raise the dead
9. Unto . . . . a child is born
10. There came three wise men . . . . the east
11. Sell . . . . thou hast, and distribute unto the poor
12. The Lamb of God, which taketh away the . . . . of the world

B.
1. . . . . am the good shepherd
2. . . . . any good thing come out of Nazareth?
3. I delight to . . . . thy will, O my God

4. . . . . have sinned, and come short of the glory of God
5. Seek those . . . . which are above
6. The gift of God is eternal life . . . . Jesus Christ our Lord
7. If any man have not the Spirit of . . . . he is none of his
8. Holiness, without . . . . no man shall see the Lord
9. Wisdom . . . . the wise more than ten mighty men (Ecclesiates 7)
10. Thou shalt have no other gods before

. . . .

7. Up by tens

TRY to fill in the missing words without looking up the Bible references.

1. The woman in the parable had TEN pieces of
   . . . . (Luke 15)
2. Paul's shipmates found the sea to be TWENTY
   . . . . deep (Acts 27)
3. Solomon's daily provision of fine flour was THIRTY
   . . . . (1 Kings 4)
4. The Children of Israel were in the wilderness for
   FORTY . . . . (Amos 2)
5. Achan stole a wedge of gold weighing FIFTY
   . . . . (Joshua 7)
6. Some of the sower's seed developed SIXTY
   . . . . (Matthew 13)
7. In Moses' day God gave His spirit to SEVENTY
   . . . . (Numbers 11)
8. During Noah's flood, it rained FORTY
   . . . . and FORTY . . . . (Genesis
   7)
9. The length of the temple in Ezekiel's vision was
   NINETY . . . . (Ezekiel 41)
10. Jesus told the story of a man who had a HUNDRED
    . . . . (Luke 15)

8. Correction!

IN each sentence cross out the wrong word and, in the space provided, write the correct one.

A.
    1. Blessed are the poor in heart: for they shall see God (Matthew 5) . . . .

    2. The wages of sin is death; but the gift of God is eternal light (Romans 6) . . . .

    3. Now abideth faith, hope, charity, these three; but the greatest of these is hope (1 Corinthians 13) . . . .

    4. He came unto his own, and his own revived him not (John 1) . . . .

    5. The Lord knoweth the way of the religious (Psalm 1) . . . .

    6. My God, my God, why hast thou forgiven me? (Matthew 27) . . . .

    7. There came wise men from the west to Jerusalem (Matthew 2) . . . .

    8. Though your sins be as scarlet, they shall be as light as snow (Isaiah 1) . . . .

    9. Wear ye one another's burdens (Galatians 6) . . . .

   10. Humble yourselves in the might of the Lord, and he shall lift you up (James 4) . . . .

B.
    1. My God shall supply all your need according to his wishes in glory (Philippians 4) . . . .

2. He that dwelleth in the secret place of the most High shall abound under the shadow of the Almighty (Psalm 91) . . . .

3. Thy shoes shall be iron and brass; and as thy ways, so shall thy strength be (Deuteronomy 33) . . . .

4. To him that knoweth to do good, and seeth it not, to him it is sin (James 4)

   . . . .

5. Let us not be weary in well doing: for in due season we shall weep, if we faint not (Galatians 6) . . . .

6. Strive to enter in the street gate (Luke 13)

   . . . .

7. Unto you that fear my name shall the Sun of righteousness arise with feeling in his wings (Malachi 4) . . . .

8. Seek ye the Lord while he may be found, call ye upon him while he is here (Isaiah 55)

   . . . .

9. Stand fast therefore in the liberty wherewith Christ hath made us see (Galatians 5)

   . . . .

10. A good game is rather to be chosen than great riches (Proverbs 22) . . . .

9. Crossword

1. Not on
4. Used with an arrow
7. Rebekah's brother
9. Needy
10. Leading up to Easter
12. Father of Ahab
14. Cain lived there
    (Genesis 4)
16. Behold
18. Plague
20. Excuse
22. Devours
23. Jacob's sons brought
    corn there
24. Part of 'to be'
25. Number of
    Commandments

DOWN

2. It happened in
   Noah's time
3. Till the soil
4. Island east of Java
5. Unit
6. Lilies neither toil nor
   do this (Matthew
   6)
8. Saint
11. Need with no end
13. Cereal
15. Lamps need it
16. Nation
17. Where the Wise Men
    saw the star
18. Leaf of a book
19. Short for ninth
    month
20. Father
21. Ever

10. Find the intruder

LET us find the intruder in each line. For example,
John would be out of place in 'Joel, Amos, Job,
Malachi, Psalms, John, Exodus', for John is not the
name of an Old Testament book.

A.   1. Agrippa, George, Herod, Ahab, David,
        Solomon
     2. Dan, Asher, Judah, Zebulun, Reuben, Moses
     3. Egypt, Italy, Israel, Malta, Australia, Syria
     4. Nile, Euphrates, Thames, Jordan, Abana,
        Pharpar
     5. Jerusalem, Rome, Caesarea, Joppa,
        Bethlehem, Madrid
     6. Apple, grape, banana, melon, fig, mulberry
     7. John, Matthew, Peter, Festus, Judas, James

B.   1. Livingstone, Carey, Moffat, Spurgeon, Cabel,
        Schweitzer
     2. Wesley, Weatherhead, Booth, Sangster,
        Churchill, Graham
     3. Baptist, Methodist, Parliament, United
        Reformed, Pentecostal, Brethren
     4. Vicar, pope, canon, senator, priest, pastor
     5. Spire, aisle, nave, porch, goal, pew
     6. Easter, Christmas, Whitsun, Ash
        Wednesday, Independence Day, Ascension
        Day
     7. Charles Wesley, Isaac Watts, Fanny Crosby,
        John Newton, William Cowper, Charles
        Dickens

C.
1. Joseph, Abel, Ruth, Jonah, Abraham, Saul
2. Love, joy, peace, hatred, goodness, faith
3. Ephesus, Smyrna, Rome, Pergamos, Thyatira, Sardis
4. Romans, Timothy, Ephesians, Matthew, Colossians, James
5. Joppa, Ptolemais, Tiberias, Tyre, Sidon, Caesarea
6. Olives, Nebo, Gerezim, Hermon, Everest, Ebal
7. Cymbal, harp, pipe, pianoforte, trumpet, timbrel

11. Crossword

1. Tree
4. Floor covering
7. She wandered with a child and a bottle (Genesis 21)
9. High temperature
10. Proud
12. Dissolve
14. Neckwear
16. Bright colour
18. '. . . to keep you from falling' (Jude)
20. Shut noisily
22. Cereals
23. One of great price in Matthew 13
24. Writing tool
25. Bird with long legs

DOWN

2. Feeling of guilt
3. How to treat evil (Psalm 97)
4. Pole on a ship
5. Limb
6. Close
8. King of Bashan (Numbers 32)
11. Employ
13. Chemistry room (abbreviated)
15. Unwell
16. Kingdom
17. Sudden rush
18. End of a prayer
19. Traditions
20. King of Egypt (2 Kings 17)
21. Mimic

12. Twelve men

EVERY word includes the letters 'men'. The answer to 'Men who are a protection' would be 'battlement'.

1. Things men wear (James 5)
2. Men who live for a minute (2 Corinthians 4)
3. Men made of small pieces (John 6)
4. Men who make an addition (Numbers 32)
5. Men who torture others (Matthew 8)
6. Men who play on 'ten strings' (Psalm 33)
7. Men who are sorrowful (John 16)
8. Men who are repairers (Mark 1)
9. Men who make references (Psalm 71)
10. Men who live in the heavens (Psalm 19)
11. Men who approve or entrust (Acts 20)
12. Men with great energy (Solomon's Songs 8)

13. Unjumble me

UNJUMBLE the following 'words' and you will have lists of names all mentioned in the Bible.

A. Apostles

1. T W E T H A M
2. N O J H
3. T R E P E
4. W A N D E R
5. P I P L I H
6. S A U D J
7. S T A M O H
8. A N E A T H L I N
9. S M A E J
10. I C O S T A I R

B. Mountains

1. A H I R M O
2. A T A R A R
3. C R A Y V A L
4. A N I S I
5. A N E H R M
6. R E A L M C
7. S O V I L E
8. I M E R G I Z
9. B O A T R
10. G O B A I L

14. Going to school

THE answer to each question can be found in the Bible book and chapter printed in the bracket.

1. Who is the head of the school? (Galatians 3)
2. What do we go to school to do? (Isaiah 1)
3. In what are our lessons printed? (John 21)
4. What do we do to understand what is in a book? (Isaiah 34)
5. What do we do very hard when preparing for an examination? (2 Timothy 2)
6. What is one called who goes to school? (1 Chronicles 25)
7. What are the class leaders called? (Proverbs 5)
8. How do we put our thoughts on paper? (Isaiah 10)
9. What do we have in our hand when we write? (Judges 5)
10. In what does a writer dip his pen? (3 John)

15. Fruit and vegetables

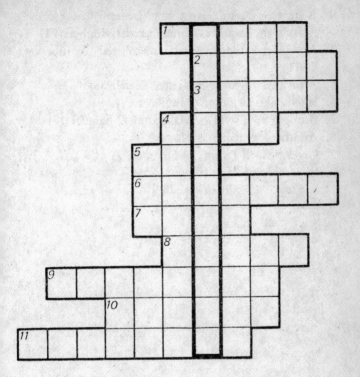

AFTER filling in the above squares you will find that the main column, reading downwards, will give you the name of yet another Bible fruit or vegetable. All names are singular.

1. A word fitly spoken is like a golden one (Proverbs 25)
2. A fig tree doesn't grow this (James 3)
3. A fruit the Israelites remembered (Numbers 11)
4. A vegetable the Israelites remembered (Numbers 11)
5. Also used to make a plaister (Isaiah 38)
6. Smells like an onion (Numbers 11)
7. Brought to David in Mahanaim (2 Samuel 17)
8. Another vegetable as No. 4
9. Gives a smell (Songs of Solomon 7)
10. In Jacob's pottage (Genesis 25)
11. It grew in a garden (Isaiah 1)

16. Not a clue

THE answer is given instead of a clue. The puzzle is to fit the words below into the open squares. Some letters are in their right squares to start you off.

A.

MATTHEW AN ART ICE YEA ACT IT
ABRAHAM HE YE ER AVERAGE RAW
EH HER EVERNEW RA RAM ARE AM

B.

HEARTEN SNAGS TRACTOR ATONE
NOTHING SHINE CRAGS NETTING

C.

WITHERS AH INSET LEAS LEANT ARE
ELI ANTEDATES ERE NED IAN ST EAT
AM SAT SPECIAL PALESTINE AS LE UR
OWE DUNE REDDISH ANEW SO DD
BOAR BROWSED

D.

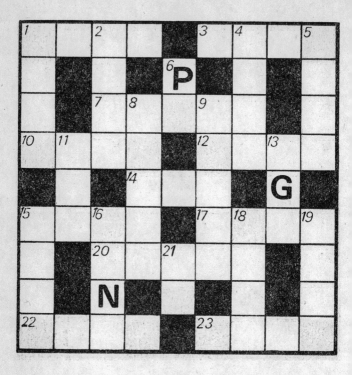

CENT GEBA IOTA EASY ANGER OMRI
PRAY TAILS PROP AYES AMOS ERASE
TRUE TROY EDEN REAR DON PI GUM
ONCE TELL LATE EGO LAMPS AM

E.

NAT HALT DEAN WON ME ABLER MOST
NO OSLO SOFAS LOT DOT OSEQ NEAR
AGENT EM MAN EBO GO DO SOLOMON
OR OG OF THE IT NED ORNAMENTS
AN WE THEM

17. Regrouping the letters

DIVIDE each 'sentence' in the correct way and you will find it becomes a text in the given chapter.

A.
1. T helor dism yshe pher dish allno tw ant (Psalm 23)
2. B less edar et hepu rein he art fort heys halls eego d (Matthew 5)
3. Foll owm ean diwi llma key ouf ish ersofm en (Matthew 4)
4. T hewag es ofs inis de athbu tt hegif tofg odi seter nall i fe (Romans 6)
5. Le tusru nwit hpatien cet her aceth atiss etbe for eus (Hebrews 12)
6. Le tth epe aceof go drul einy ourh ear ts (Colossians 3)
7. Be ary eon eanot her sbur den sand soful filt hela wofch rist (Galatians 6)

B.
1. Go diso ur refu geands treng thave rypre sent he lpint rouble (Psalm 46)
2. Thyw ordis ala mpun tomyfe etan daligh tunt omyp ath (Psalm 119)
3. Het hatdwe llethint hese cretpla ceoft hemos thig hsha llabi deun derth esha dowoft heal mig hty (Psalm 91)
4. Asof tans wert urn ethaw aywr ath (Proverbs 15)
5. Ago odna meis rat hert obech osenth angre atri ches (Proverbs 22)

6. Re memb ern owth ycre at orinth eda ysoft hyyo uth (Ecclesiastes 12)
7. Prep arey eth ewa yofth elor dmak estra igh tint hedes ertah ighwa yforo urg od (Isaiah 40)

18. Crossword

1. Not quite all
2. Open in poetic form
5. Upon
7. Outcast
9. Spoil
11. Egypt is part of it
13. Nebuchadnezzar's capital
16. Gaelic language
17. Girl's name
18. Paul left there for Antioch (Acts 14)
20. Australian bird
21. Tree
23. Paul's companion
26. Belonging to
27. Gave food
28. Either

DOWN

1. Gift
2. Animal
3. Sympathy
4. Starts many Spanish names
6. Neither
7. Sent with Timothy to Macedonia (Acts 19)
8. She had quarrelled with Syntyche (Philippians 4)
10. Father of Isaac
12. Indian coins
14. Gamble
15. Mixed measurement of length
19. On which a wheel revolves
20. Self
22. Not him
24. On condition
25. Advertisement

19. A choice of three

TICK the right ones

A.
1. Who was left-handed? (Esau, Ehud, Eli)
2. On which mountain were the Ten Commandments given to Moses? (Sinai, Zion, Nebo)
3. Who was Queen of Ethiopia? (Cana, Candace, Canaan)
4. Which was a pool in Jerusalem? (Bethesda, Bethsaida, Bethshan)
5. Who wrote in a book for Jeremiah? (Barak, Baruch, Balak)
6. Who was Governor of Syria? (Cornelius, Cyrenius, Sergius)
7. With whom did Paul leave a cloak? (Caleb, Carmel, Carpus)
8. Where did the Israelites find twelve wells of water? (Elim, Elam, Elath)
9. What mighty man of valour reduced his army from 32,000 to 300? (Gideon, Gibeon, Gibeah)
10. Who was an eloquent Jew? (Apollonia, Apollos, Apollyon)

B.
1. Who was the father of harpists and organists? (Jabal, Jubal, Jabez)
2. What was the name of Rebekah's father? (Lamech, Laban, Lydia)

3. Where did Dagon fall on his face? (Ashdod, Ashima, Asher)
4. Who left Paul bound to show 'the Jews a pleasure'? (Felix, Festus, Fortunatus)
5. Who was the father of Samson? (Manoah, Manasseh, Moriah)
6. Who was one of David's harpists? (Azaniah, Azaziah, Azariah)
7. Which was the early name for Bethel? (Buz, Huz, Luz)
8. On which island was John exiled? (Patmos, Paphos, Pathros)
9. Who blessed Jesus in the Temple? (Simeon, Solomon, Samson)
10. Where was Paul born? (Tarshish, Tarsus, Tarah)

C. 1. When did Augustine land in England? (AD 1066, AD 597, 55 BC)
2. Who founded the Methodist Church? (Charles Wesley, Marquis of Wellesley, John Wesley)
3. When Jesus was on earth, where did He live? (Holy Grail, Holy Land, Holy Island)
4. Who wrote the hymn 'Lead, kindly light'? (John Newman, John Mill, John Milton)
5. Where was John Wesley born? (Tamworth, Epworth, Walworth)
6. Who carved the famous statue of David? (Fra Angelico, Michelangelo, Normal Angell)

7. Where did Sir Wilfred Grenfell work as a missionary doctor? (Labrador, Ecuador, Salvador)

8. Who was a missionary to Calabar in Africa? (Mary Jones, Mary Slessor, Mary Moffat)

9. Who is associated with Glastonbury, England? (Joseph, son of Jacob, Joseph of Nazareth, Joseph of Arimathea)

10. What people make pilgrimages to Mecca? (Buddists, Hindus, Mohammedans)

D.
1. Who was a king of Egypt? (Nebo, Nero, Necho)

2. Where did Paul go to soon after his conversion? (Arabah, Arabia, Ararat)

3. What was the name of one of Naomi's daughters-in-law? (Mizpah, Rizpah, Orpah)

4. Which gate leads to life? (Broad, narrow, crooked)

5. The giving of what kind of water is an act of love? (Clean, living, cold)

6. Which way did the writer of Psalm 119 choose? (Pleasantness, truth, escape)

7. What was the name of Joshua's father? (Nod, Nob, Nun)

8. Who was the first Christian convert in Europe? (Lydia, Lybia, Lydda)

9. Who was wounded by Peter in Gethsemane?
   (Malachi, Malchus, Malluch)
10. What was the name of a son of Shem? (Lot,
    Lod, Lud)

E. 1. Who worked to reform English prisons?
      (John Milton, John Howard, John
      Williams)
   2. Who preached to the birds? (Francis of
      Assisi, Francis Burleigh, Francis Xavier)
   3. Who worked to help starving, ill-treated
      children? (Sir Ernest Shackleton, William
      Shakespeare, Lord Shaftesbury)
   4. Who taught that every Christian should be
      an imitator of Christ? (Thomas à Kempis,
      Thomas à Beckett, Thomas de Quincey)
   5. What is the motto of The Salvation Army?
      (Be prepared, Blood and Fire, In God we
      trust)
   6. Who wrote the hymn, 'O for a closer walk
      with God'? (William Henry Parker,
      William Cowper, William Walsham
      How)
   7. When was Isaac Watts the hymn-writer
      born? (1674, 1774, 1874)
   8. Who worked for forty years among the
      fishermen of Labrador (Richard Grenville,
      Wilfred Grenfell, John Greenleaf Whittier)

9. Who was a missionary doctor to India?
   (Martin Luther, Henry Martin, Martin
   Luther King)
10. Who inspired the beginning of the British
    and Foreign Bible Society? (Mary Slessor,
    Mary Moffat, Mary Jones)

20. Crossword

ACROSS

1. Abel's brother
4. Light period
6. Paper money
7. Untie or unpack

9. Neither
10. Source of electricity
12. Father
13. Also
17. Dirty mark
19. Extinct bird
21. Observe
22. Father (Hebrew)
24. Human being
25. Young man (1,3)

DOWN

1. Friend
2. Country in Asia
3. Midday
4. Daniel was thrown into one
5. Story
8. Short sleep
11. Rested
14. Of the nose
15. Expire
16. First man
17. Cry softly
18. Want
20. Tribe of Israel
23. University degree

21. Women of the Bible

IF you add the missing letters you will have the names of ten women mentioned in the Bible.

1. . I . I A .
2. . E . O R . .
3. . B . G . I .
4. . L I . . B . . H
5. . E . E . E .
6. . R I . C . . L .
7. . E . I . A H
8. . A . T . A
9. . O . N . A
10. . E . O . I . S

22. Five-letter words

FILL in the squares according to the clues by the side of each line. The first letter of the second word is the same as the last of the first word, and so on.

A.

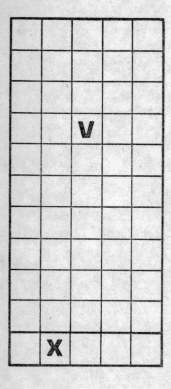

1. Even
2. Let alone
3. Where Saul found a witch (1 Samuel 28)
4. Large stream of water
5. 'The heathen . . . the kingdoms were moved (Psalm 46)
6. The Lord lays it in storehouses (Psalm 33)
7. Where people live
8. Find the answer
9. He walked with God (Genesis 5)
10. Divide into two parts
11. Praise

		E		
	R			

B.

1. Seller of purple (Acts 16)
2. It is outrageous (Proverbs 27)
3. Circles
4. Hurry
5. Watercourse
6. 'Moses' hands were . . . ' (Exodus 17)
7. Not old
8. Place of burial
9. Wrong
10. Royal

1. Mother of Ishmael
2. Group of mountains
3. It mounts up at
   God's command
   (Job 39)
4. Keen
5. Machine man
6. Gas measurement
7. Creator
8. Large meeting
9. Surrender
10. From the Netherlands

D.
1. King of Judea
2. The Wise Men and Pilate's wife had one
3. Played by an orchestra
4. Room in a ship
5. 'I will . . . leave thee, not forsake thee' (Hebrews 13)
6. Kingly
7. According to law
8. Hiram was always this to David (1 Kings 5)
9. Entangle
10. Door fastener

23. Crossword

ACROSS

1. Wizards do this
(Isaiah 8)
3. Image
7. Paul hoped to visit
here (Romans 15)
10. Speed
12. Jewels

14. Knowledge
15. Son of Ishmael
    (Genesis 25)
17. King of Israel
20. Son of Enan
    (Numbers 1)
22. . . . it not in Gath
    (2 Samuel 1)
23. Island off west coast
    of Scotland

DOWN

1. Not rich
2. This wind breaks
   ships (Psalm 48)
4. Sandy ground
5. Not gain
6. Mother
8. He slew 120,000
   soldiers in a day (2
   Chronicles 28)
9. Almost take no
   notice
11. Wonder
13. Spoil
15. Portable house
16. Goliath was armed
    with this coat
18. Second Gospel
19. Island
21. Singular of are

24. Nine lives of a cat

EVERY word includes the letters 'cat'. The answer to 'a place to find a cat' would be 'location'. The Bible reference following the clue is the book and chapter in which the answer appears.

1. The cat who has a calling (Ephesians 4)
2. ,, ,, ,, makes a prayer (Psalm 6)
3. ,, ,, ,, gets the message over (Galatians 6)
4. ,, ,, ,, is unhealthy (Isaiah 47)
5. ,, ,, ,, spreads itself around (Matthew 9)
6. ,, ,, ,, lives on a farm or on the hills (Psalm 50)
7. ,, ,, ,, is part of forgiveness (Romans 4)
8. ,, ,, ,, is a fisher of men (Luke 5)
9. ,, ,, ,, was part of a feast (John 10)

25. Mini-crosswords

A.

ACROSS: 1. He slept in an ark of bulrushes; 4. For
. . . . in the kingdom.

DOWN: 1. A high hill; 2. The Ten Commandments
were given here; 3. On what were the Ten
Commandments written?

B.

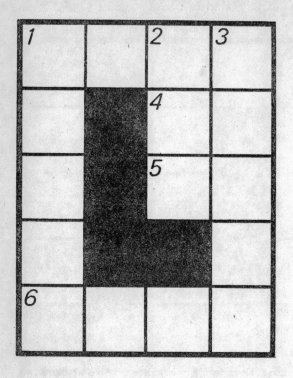

ACROSS: 1. The moon has . . . . brightness than the sun; 4. Exclamation; 5. Not from; 6. Jesus is the . . . . light.

DOWN: 1. We should walk in this; 2. The people who . . . . in darkness saw a great light (Matthew 4); 3. The glory of the Lord did this around the Bethlehem shepherds.

C.

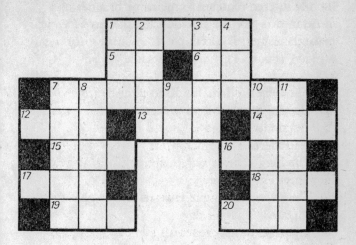

ACROSS: 1. Worship; 5. 'And . . . . I am with you alway (Matthew 28); 6. Birthplace of Abraham; 7. Where Peter's mother-in-law was ill (Mark 1); 12. What Bartimeus did by the wayside (Mark 10); 13. Old cloth or rough fun; 14. Negative; 15. Cut grass; 16. Rahab did this with two spies; 17. Daniel was here with lions; 18. How many loaves did David take to his brothers? (1 Samuel 17); 19. Allow; 20. A false god (Jeremiah 50)

DOWN: 1. Swiss mountain; 2. A worker, not just a hearer (James 1); 3. Step; 4. Period; 7. Ship of the desert; 8. Make at one; 9. Royal Academy; 10. Bind; 11. Example

26. Hidden people

HIDDEN in each sentence is the name of a person
mentioned in the Bible. Underline the letters which
make the names. For example, Is a nomad a man who
wanders about? This gives the name 'Adam'.

1. Though all others fail, God remains true
2. He sang a solo Monday evening
3. Onesimus is called a beloved brother
4. He rode in a chariot
5. The king chose a wise helper
6. Amos eschewed evil
7. They were all simple villagers
8. Sunday is a sacred day
9. The rope terminated with a knot
10. The women came very early to the garden

27. Hidden places

HIDDEN in each sentence is the name of a place mentioned in the Bible. Underline the letters which make the names. For example, An heroic a nation as Israel. This gives the name 'Cana'.

1. In Damascus is a really straight street
2. There is no doubt about God's love
3. He may wander because he has lost his way
4. We can always be sure of God's presence
5. The Bible is urgently needed by all people
6. He made an instrument and called it a lyre
7. Peter eased the man's pain completely
8. The letter came in an opened envelope
9. The sea has many misty regions
10. Will the Magi be on the road to Jerusalem?

28. Changing letters

CHANGE one letter at a time to find an opposite word.

A. W A G E

. . . .	something made for sale (Nehemiah 10)
. . . .	a skin blemish
. . . .	sweep of a bird's wing
. . . .	it's flat and floats
. . . .	a chasm
. . . .	something for nothing

B. P O O R

. . . .	a small pond
. . . .	a human head; number of votes
. . . .	it eases pain
. . . .	a heap
. . . .	irritate
. . . .	eaten by Indians
. . . .	wealthy

C. S E E D

. . . .	to give food
. . . .	a boy's name
. . . .	at liberty
. . . .	planted by the rivers of water (Psalm 1)

D. S A N D

. . . . went down in water
. . . . a column
. . . . a shelf
. . . . water came from it in Horeb
       (Exodus 17)

29. Writing by numbers

WRITE the answers, letter by letter, in the numbered squares below and you will be able to read a well-known verse of the Bible. The answer to 'frozen water' has three letters. They are to be written in squares 16 15 7—in that order.

A. 1. Not a national or native (Deut. 15:3) 12 21 4
        25 8 3 18 26 22
    2. They keep the hands warm 1 11 13 20 10
    3. Frozen water (Psalm
        147:17) 16 15 7
    4. Sailing vessel 2 5 6 24 23
    5. Building place 9 14 19 17

B. 1. Small javelin (Job 41:26) 14 15 2 8
   2. Rules . . . 13 10 6 20 7 4
   3. Not cold . . . 9 12 5
   4. Noisy . . . 11 21 3 17
   5. Small point . . . 18 22 1
   6. Land where Cain went (Genesis 4:16) . . . 16
      19 23

C.
1. . . . in the balances (Daniel 5:27) . . . 17 6 1 9 5 16 21
2. Stronghold . . . 13 18 19 14
3. Small mountain . . . 10 8 20 7
4. 'My heart was . . . within me (Psalm 39:3) . . . 15 12 4
5. Small carpet . . . 3 2 11

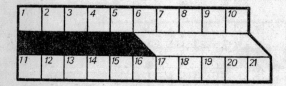

30. An escape is planned

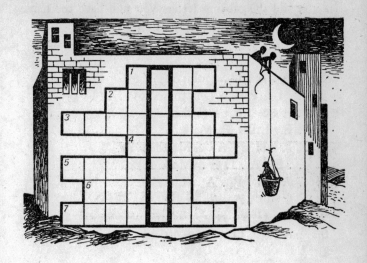

SOLVE the following clues and write the answers in the squares above. You will find that the letters in the thickened column are all the same.

1. He escaped in a basket (Acts 9)
2. He fled to the tabernacle (1 Kings 2)
3. He escaped with eight men (Jeremiah 41)
4. He escaped through a window (1 Samuel 19)
5. He ran away for fear of his brother (Judges 9)
6. He fled from the presence of the Lord and found himself inside a big fish
7. He escaped on a horse (1 Kings 20)

31. Men in the Gospels

IF you add the missing letters you will have the name of ten men mentioned in the Gospels.

1. . A . A . U S (John 11)
2. . . I A P . . S (Matthew 26)
3. . A . A . B . S (Luke 23)
4. . E . E D . E (Mark 3)
5. . R . H E . A . S Matthew 2)
6. . . E . A . D E . (Mark 15)
7. . A . H . R . A . (Luke 1)
8. . L . O . A . (John 19)
9. . A . H A . A . . (John 1)
10. . A . T . O . O . E . (Mark 3)

32. Scramble

BUILD up Bible names in the squares provided by starting each name with one of the larger letters, using each letter once only. Write the answers in the rows of squares and you will find that the blackened squares read downwards will give you the same name as the top or second row.

A. New Testament men

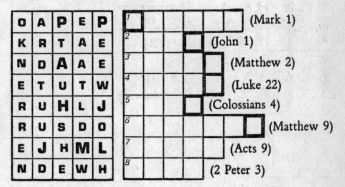

O	A	P	E	P
K	R	T	A	E
N	D	A	A	E
E	T	U	T	W
R	U	H	L	J
R	U	S	D	O
E	J	H	M	L
N	D	E	W	H

1. (Mark 1)
2. (John 1)
3. (Matthew 2)
4. (Luke 22)
5. (Colossians 4)
6. (Matthew 9)
7. (Acts 9)
8. (2 Peter 3)

B. Old Testament men

S	A	O	E	J
Z	A	R	O	D
A	H	U	Z	E
O	A	M	M	H
H	A	B	S	E
A	S	L	A	L
U	N	O	A	I
R	A	M	H	K

1. (Genesis 2)
2. (Psalm 47)
3. (Nehemiah 8)
4. (1 Samuel 24)
5. (Exodus 17)
6. (Proverbs 25)
7. (1 Kings 1)

C. More Old Testament men

A	C	A	S	D
H	M	O	J	H
A	N	I	A	J
L	I	A	E	L
O	I	D	U	L
E	B	S	O	D
M	E	E	E	I
S	V	L	A	N

1. (Ezekiel 28)
2. (1 Samuel 16)
3. (Genesis 6)
4. (1 Kings 17)
5. (Joshua 1)
6. (1 Samuel 1)
7. (Genesis 27)
8. (Psalm 99)

D. Women of the Bible

T	E	L	S	Y
R	M	H	N	A
A	A	H	Y	H
A	I	A	H	A
A	N	H	D	R
E	R	A	S	A
R	D	A	R	C
M	A	O	V	G

1. (Genesis 21)
2. (Matthew 2)
3. (Acts 9)
4. (Genesis 16)
5. (Luke 10)
6. (1 Samuel 1)
7. (Genesis 3)
8. (Acts 16)

33. Crossword

ACROSS

1. Steal
3. Footwear
6. Pain
7. Animal
8. Girl's name

10. Not down
11. Sounds like 'or'
12. Where the Israelites
    lived in Egypt
16. Main street
19. Assistant
20. Fetter
21. We do this with a
    race

DOWN

1. Thick string
2. Purse
3. Jesus was a good one
4. Edge of a garment
5. He was a hunter
   (Genesis 25)
9. God made him in His
   image
10. You and I
13. Musical instrument
14. Elijah ran before him
    (1 Kings 18)
15. First garden
17. Achan did this
    with his spoils
    (Joshua 7)
18. Over

34. God's written word

IN the year 1800 a poor Welsh girl walked 25 miles
barefoot to buy a Bible. The initial letters of the
answers to the following questions will tell you what
was formed as a result of this four years later.

1. To what Welsh town did Mary Jones walk to
     buy her first Bible?
2. To what country did William Carey take the
     word of God?
3. In Paul's travels, where were the people specially
     known for their Bible study? (Acts 17)
4. What is the word of God to our feet? (Psalm
     119)
5. For how long will the word of the Lord endure?
     (1 Peter 1)
6. How many books are there in the Bible?
7. About whom was the Epistle to Philemon
     written?
8. Ten of what did Moses write on stone?
9. What is the missing word in this verse? 'Scripture
     is given by . . . of God' (2 Timothy 3)
10. What is a Bible letter called?
11. How many are there of the last question?
12. From what age had the young ruler kept the
     commandments? (Matthew 19)

35. Simon

WRITE in the squares provided the name or word associated with each Simon; for example, Simon, sorcerer, as in Acts 8:9. You will discover something special about the thickened column.

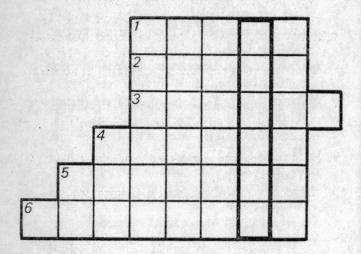

1. Brother of Andrew (Luke 6)
2. He lived in Bethany (Matthew 26)
3. He carried the Cross of Jesus (Matthew 27)
4. He lived in Joppa (Acts 9)
5. An apostle, but not the fisherman (Luke 6)
6. Jesus sat down to meat in his house (Luke 7)

36. A ten of 'A's

WRITE the answers in a column below the clues. As you proceed you will notice something strange about the beginnings and endings of the names.

1. Who was the father of Elisheba? (Exodus 6)
2. Who fled after David? (1 Samuel 22)
3. He was a king in Paul's day (2 Corinthians 11)
4. A city grouped with Libnah and Ether (Joshua 15)
5. Who gave Paul his sight in Damascus? (Acts 9)
6. Who was master of Nebuchadnezzar's eunuchs? (Daniel 1)
7. What king was struck with leprosy? (2 Kings 15)
8. He was a prince over Solomon's household (1 Kings 4)
9. He was a Jebusite and owned a threshing floor (2 Samuel 24)
10. His hand was with Jeremiah (Jeremiah 26)

37. Bible insects

AFTER filling in the squares below you will find that the main column, reading downwards, will give you the name of yet another Bible insect.

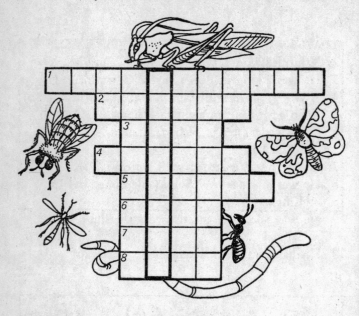

1. It shall be a burden (Ecclesiastes 12)
2. God will restore the years it has eaten (Joel 2)
3. Neither this nor rust will corrupt in heaven (Matthew 6)
4. It drove away two Amorite kings (Joshua 24)
5. It is in kings' palaces (Proverbs 30)
6. Aaron made it from dust (Exodus 8)
7. It killed a gourd (Jonah 4)
8. Blind guides strain it (Matthew 23)

38. Paul's travels

TAKE two groups of letters at a time, join them together, and you will have eight names in each puzzle, names of places visited by Paul.

A.

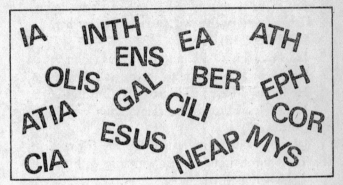

IA INTH EA ATH
ENS BER EPH
OLIS GAL CILI COR
ATIA ESUS NEAP MYS
CIA

B.

CYP RGA SAL HOS
TRA IOCH
UCIA SELE
ICO RUS LYS
AMIS PAP
ANT PE NIUM

39. Bible surgery

WRITE the answers in a column below the clues and you will find that the initial letters of answers 1 to 7 spell the answer to clue 8.

1. Purge me with this and I shall be clean (Psalm 51)
2. There were twelve wells of clean water here (Exodus 15)
3. Jesus did this to a blind man's eyes (John 9)
4. Jesus sent a cured one to the priest (Matthew 8)
5. He foretold Hezekiah's recovery (2 Kings 20)
6. Where Jesus brought a widow's son back to life (Luke 7)
7. Jesus cast out an unclean spirit here (Mark 5)
8. The Sun of righteousness will arise with this in his wings (Malachi 4)

40. At the seaside

TURN to the Bible book and chapter mentioned after each clue, then write in a circle the number of the verse which includes the name of the part of the drawing.

1. Paul's companions took these up (Acts 27)
2. Good weather when red at night (Matthew 16)
3. Some people make this of faith (1 Timothy 1)
4. They beat on the ship where Jesus slept (Mark 4)
5. When Simon let it down, it broke (Luke 5)
6. Andrew was one (Matthew 4)
7. Made of fine linen and broidered (Ezekiel 27)
8. God weighs these in a balance (Isaiah 40)
9. Soldiers cut the ropes from this (Acts 27)
10. Paul might have fallen on these (Acts 27)

41. Making the trio

ADD the third word in each Bible trio

1. Gold, frankincense. . . . .(Matthew 2)
2. Peter, James. . . . .(Matthew 17)
3. Hebrew, Greek. . . . .(John 19)
4. Faith, hope. . . . .(1 Corinthians 13)
5. Shem, Ham. . . . .(Genesis 7)
6. Sun, moon. . . . .(Genesis 1)
7. Love, joy. . . . .(Galatians 5)
8. Mount, run. . . . .(Isaiah 40)
9. Kingdom, power. . . . .(Matthew 6)
10. Blind, halt. . . . .(John 5)

42. Building a house

TURN to the Bible book and chapter mentioned after each clue, then write in a circle the number of the verse which includes the name of the part of the building.

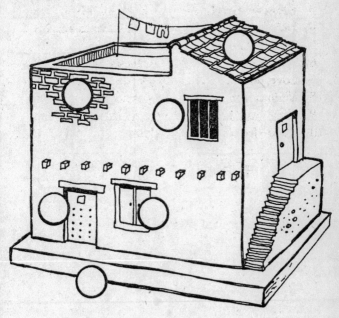

1. The mother of Sisera looked out through one (Judges 5)
2. Uncovered by four friends (Mark 2)
3. To be shut for prayer (Matthew 6)
4. Should be laid on a rock (Luke 6)
5. No more straw was given to make it (Exodus 5)
6. Where the disciples awaited Pentecost (Acts 1)

43. Places and people of the Acts

REARRANGE each line in the correct order and the centre line downwards will give you a Bible name.

A.

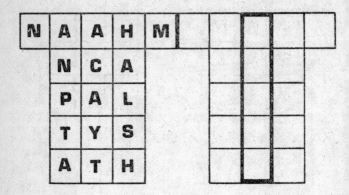

Key: an island visited by Paul

B.

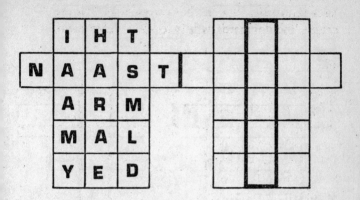

I	H	T

N	A	A	S	T

A	R	M

M	A	L

Y	E	D

Key: Country where Paul died

C.

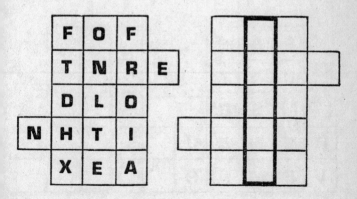

F	O	F

T	N	R	E

D	L	O

N	H	T	I

X	E	A

Key: Governor in Caesarea

D.

	L	I	L	
S	Y	D	A	
	D	A	O	
	M	T	N	I
	A	L	D	

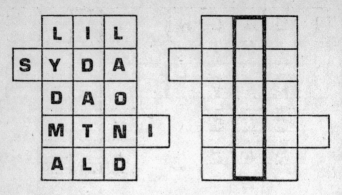

Key: Seller of purple

E.

	S	A	S	
	C	A	T	
	M	E	G	
H	E	N	A	V
L	E	M	A	R

Key: Had seven sons, all exorcists

86

F.

E	O	A	S	H					
	N	T	I						
	M	A	Y						
	O	N	S						
	N	A	T						

Key: Tanner in Joppa

G.

P	E	E	R	L					
	E	H	N						
S	H	A	M	R					
	G	E	A						
	A	R	T						

Key: Town in Pamphylia

44. Building a text

A.

B.

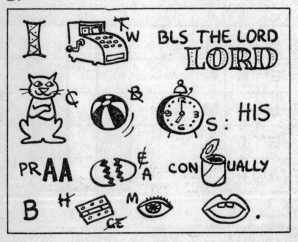

C.

H Y T   UPON
S

THE   S : 4   OHTU

E A   4T   FIND IT   ER

Y   - CALENDAR -

D.

N L   US   I W / H T

N T   IENCE   THE   F R

B TH IS 6 +IX ET B4 US.

E.

H C N, TH

F D, NYTHR W H

F ERED TI/ON THE OF THE

R TH GOD H PRE ED

4 THEM & TH D/L HIM.

F.

D G VED; R G

IS R/N L/M ED; 4

WHATSOEVER A B·S ETH,

T C HE B SO

Ł P.

45. Soldier in armour

AFTER each chapter number in the clues write the number of the verse which names the part of the armour or of the soldier.

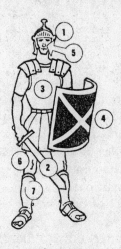

1. It must be of salvation (Isaiah 59: . . . .)
2. It is the word of God (Ephesians 6: . . . .)
3. Standing for love and faith (1 Thessalonians 5: . . . .)
4. The Lord is this to his followers (Psalm 33: . . . .)
5. It's boldness will be changed (Ecclesiastes 8: . . . .)
6. When feeble, they need confirming (Isaiah 35: . . . .)
7. Goliath wore these on his legs (1 Samuel 17: . . . .)

46. Wives and . . .

EACH answer contains the letters 'and'. Write the
answers in a column below the clues and you will
find that the initial letters answer the clue: 'They look
after wives'. These letters also complete the heading of
the puzzle.

1. The widow of Zarephath had this amount of oil
   (1 Kings 17)
2. A man of this quality has wisdom (Proverbs 10)
3. Peter bound these on in prison (Acts 12)
4. It was 'plucked out of the fire' (Zechariah 3)
5. Peter's brother and patron saint of Scotland
6. Fifteen letters meaning 'in spite of' in Exodus 16
   and Revelation 2
7. Herod ' . . . of them where Jesus should be born'
   (Matthew 2)
8. One who utters this is a fool (Proverbs 10)

47. God created

THE Bible tells us that God created all living things. Write downwards in the columns the names of eight of the 'living things' in the drawing and you will find that the letters along the top of the columns spell the name of the remaining one.

48. All directions

WORDS are spelt forwards, backwards, upwards, downwards or diagonally. Loop each word as in the example in puzzle A.

A. Jesus said: 'I am . . . ' then followed words such as the 'truth'. Eight of these words are in this puzzle.

M	W	A	H	B	G	Q	N
W	A	T	E	R	O	V	R
I	Y	H	B	E	F	I	L
P	C	G	F	A	T	N	S
K	L	I	G	D	D	E	U
V	E	L	O	W	X	J	C
Z	A	O	T	R	U	T	H
E	R	Y	B	F	I	D	H

B. The names of seven Bible metals are hidden here.

R	N	B	U	F	P	Z	B
G	O	L	D	B	S	C	R
A	R	E	P	P	O	C	A
K	I	E	H	T	G	D	S
Q	D	C	V	E	V	J	S
F	D	A	E	L	A	Y	L
W	O	E	X	T	I	N	M
I	G	N	H	I	J	S	K

C. The names of eight Bible trees are hidden here.

S	F	R	B	S	D	P	D
A	Y	H	J	L	N	X	N
F	U	C	E	D	A	R	O
L	I	Y	A	G	K	W	M
C	T	G	A	M	A	F	L
E	V	I	L	O	O	I	A
M	O	A	B	E	C	R	D
Q	P	Z	A	K	V	E	E

49. Baking day

WRITE the answers in the squares provided. All the words are Bible words and all the letters in the thickened squares are vowels. When read downwards, these vowels make an interesting pattern.

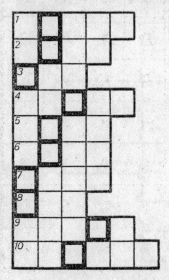

1. The most important liquid
2. Seasons and preserves
3. Crack the shell before using
4. Called the 'staff of life'
5. Cows and goats give this
6. Where Bible women ground their corn
7. Baking place
8. In Bible days it came from the olive tree
9. Basis of bread
10. Left-over pieces

50. Old Testament prophets

AFTER filling in the above squares you will find that the main column, reading downwards, will give you the name of yet another Old Testament prophet.

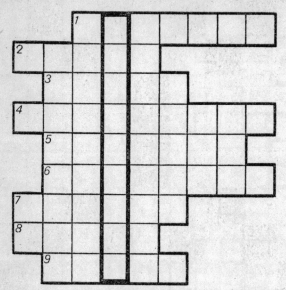

1. A priest whose prophecy has forty-eight chapters
2. First of the minor prophets
3. He prophesied Bethlehem as the birthplace of Jesus (see Matthew 2:6 in a reference Bible)
4. With the main column, the longest name for a writing prophet
5. Prophecy begins with 'The vision of . . .'
6. A mournful prophet
7. He was imprisoned with lions
8. He travelled inside a large fish
9. He began his prophecy with a 'burden'

51. Crossword

1. This day is the
   Sabbath
7. French for 'and'
9. Organ of the body
11. Father backwards
12. Base

14. He wrote his visions in a book (2 Chronicles 9)
16. Give him this and he'll take a mile
17. Made from soap
18. Quote
19. A twisted belt
20. Water taps
21. Boy's name shortened
23. Starts many Bible names; means 'God'
26. He found Livingstone

DOWN

2. Used to be
3. Period
4. In the direction of
5. Town of Zacchaeus
6. Close follower of Jesus
8. Pick-me-up
9. Air
10. He is . . . (Easter)
11. Muddle
13. Short month
15. Make into a knight
22. Possess
24. Saint
25. Myself

Answers

1. It's in the Bible

1 Saul (v. 20)   2 Canaan (v. 8)   3 Nazareth (v.
23)   4 Cain (v. 9)   5 Paul (v. 52)   6 Titus (1:15)
7 Jesus (v. 6)   8 Harmless (v. 16)   9 Daniel (5: 27)
10 Pharisees (vv. 12–14)   Extra: Scriptures (v.15)

2. Crossword

ACROSS: 1 Imp   3 See   5 Ed   6 Uni   7 La
9 Zoar   11 Tomb   13 LSD   14 Kite   15 Mica
16 Too   17 Ears   20 Anna   33 LC   23 Urn
24 AM   25 Eon   26 Sag

DOWN: 1 Ido   2 Purse   3 Sit   4 Elm   5 Ezekiel
8 Abraham   10 Altar   12 Orion   15 Moans
18 Ace   19 Sun   21 Nag

3. Miracles and wonders

A. 1 Capernaum   2 Galilee   3 Siloam   4 Bethany
    5 Nain   6 Jericho   7 Nazareth   8 Gadarenes
    9 Bethsaida

B. 1 Jordan   2 Marah   3 Zarephath   4 Rephidim
    5 Ajalon   6 Pharoah   7 Carmel
    8 Darius   9 Nineveh

4. Squared off

A. Courage
B. Almighty
C. Testimony
D. Revelation
E. Extortioner
F. Intercession
G. Forgetfulness

5. Crossword

ACROSS: 1 Not 4 Hit 7 Peter 9 Amen
11 Mars 13 Dan 15 Noe 16 Pop 18 An 19 Ai
21 Galatians 25 Enoch 26 Foe 27 Ear

DOWN: 2 Open 3 Ten 4 Hem 5 Iran 6 Mad
8 Use 10 Manna 12 Roman 14 No 16 Plane
17 Price 18 Age 20 Ise (Or Ism, or Ist) 22 Leo
23 To 24 Aha

6. Filling the gap

A. The blood of Jesus Christ his Son cleanseth us
from all sin (1 John 1:7)
B. I can do all things through Christ which
strengtheneth me (Philippians 4: 13)

7. Up by tens

1 Silver (v. 8)   2 Fathoms (v. 28)   3 Measures
(v. 22)   4 Years (v. 10)   5 Shekels (v. 21)   6 Fold
(v. 8)   7 Elders (v. 25)   8 Days, nights (v. 12)
9 Cubits (v. 12)   10 Sheep (v. 4)

8. Correction!

A. 1 Poor/Pure (v. 8)   2 Light/Life (v. 23)
   3 Hope/Charity (v. 13)   4 Revived/Received
   (v. 11)   5 Religious/Righteous (v. 6)
   6 Forgiven/Forsaken (v. 46)   7 West/East
   (v.1)   8 Light/White (v. 18)   9 Wear/Bear
   (v. 2)   10 Might/Sight (v. 10)

B. 1 Wishes/Riches (v. 19)   2 Abound/Abide
   (v. 1)   3 Ways/Days (v. 25)   4 Seeth/Doeth
   (v. 17)   5 Weep/Reap (v. 9)   6 Street/Strait
   (v. 24)   7 Fealing/Healing (v. 2)   8 Here/Near
   (v. 6)   9 Sea/Free (v. 1)   10 Game/Name
   (v. 1)

9. Crossword

ACROSS: 1 Off   4 Bow   7 Laban   9 Poor
10 Lent   12 Omri   14 Nod   16 See   18 Pest
20 Plea   22 Eats   23 Egypt   24 Are   25 Ten
DOWN: 2 Flood   3 Farm   4 Bali   5 One   6 Spin
8 St   11 Nee(d)   13 Rye   15 Oil   16 State
17 East   18 Page   19 Sept   20 Pa   21 Eer

10. Find the intruder

A.
1. George (not a king in the Bible)
2. Moses (not a son of Jacob)
3. Australia (not a country mentioned in the Bible)
4. Thames (not a Bible river)
5. Madrid (not a Bible town)
6. Banana (not a Bible fruit)
7. Festus (not a disciple of Jesus)

B.
1. Spurgeon (not a missionary)
2. Churchill (not a preacher)
3. Parliament (not a church)
4. Senator (not a church office)
5. Goal (not part of a church)
6. Independence Day (not a church festival)
7. Charles Dickens (not a hymn-writer)

C.
1. Ruth (not a man)
2. Hatred (not a fruit of the Spirit — Galatians 5: 22, 23)
3. Rome (not one of the seven churches in Revelation 1–3)
4. Matthew (not an Epistle)
5. Tiberias (not on the Mediterranean coast)
6. Everest (not a Bible mountain)
7. Pianoforte (not a Bible instrument)

11. Crossword

ACROSS: 1 Ash 4 Mat 7 Hagar 9 Heat
10 Smug 12 Melt 14 Tie 16 Red 18 Able
20 Slam 22 Oats 23 Pearl 24 Pen 25 Emu

DOWN: 2 Shame 3 Hate 4 Mast 5 Arm
6 Shut 8 Og 11 Use 13 Lab 15 Ill 16 Realm
17 Dash 18 Amen 19 Lore 20 So 21 Ape

12. Twelve men

1 Garments (v. 2) 2 Moment (v. 17) 3 Fragments
(v. 12) 4 Augment (v. 14) 5 Torment (v. 29)
6 Instrument (v. 2) 7 Lament (v. 20) 8 Mend (or
mending) (v. 19) 9 Mention (v. 16) 10 Firmament
(v. 1) Commend (v. 32) 12 Vehement (v. 6)

13. Unjumble me

A. 1 Matthew 2 John 3 Peter 4 Andrew
    5 Philip 6 Judas 7 Thomas 8 Nathaniel
    9 James 10 Iscariot
B. 1 Morash 2 Ararat 3 Calvary 4 Sinai
    5 Herman 6 Carmel 7 Olives 8 Gerizim
    9 Tabor 10 Gilboa

14.   Going to school

1 Schoolmaster (v. 24)   2 Learn (v. 17)   3 Books
(v. 25)   4 Read (v. 16)   5 Study (v. 15)   6 Scholar
(v. 8)   7 Teachers (v. 13)   8 Write (v.19)   9 Pen
(v. 14)   10 Ink (v. 13)

15.   Fruit and vegetables

1 Apple (v. 11)   2 Olive (v. 12)   3 Melon (v. 5)
4 Leek (v. 5)   5 Fig (v. 21)   6 Garlick (v. 5)
7 Bean (v. 28)   8 Onion   9 Mandrake (v. 13)
10 Lentil (v. 34)   11 Cucumber (v. 8)
Main column: Pomegranate

16.   Not a clue

A. ACROSS: 1 Abraham   6 Are   7 Er   9 It
10 Raw   11 Act   12 Am   14 Eh   15 Yea
17 Evernew

DOWN: 1 Average   2 Ra   3 Art   4 He
5 Matthew   8 Ram   9 Ice   13 Her   15 Ye
16 An

B. ACROSS: 1 Atone   6 Hearten   7 Nothing
8 Crags
DOWN: 2 Tractor   3 Netting   4 Shine   5 Snags

C. ACROSS: 1 Browsed 5 So 6 Ur
8 Palestine 12 Ere 13 Ned 14 Am
15 As 16 Ian 19 Eli 21 Antedates 24 Le
25 Ah 26 Withers
DOWN: 1 Boar 2 Owe 3 Sat 4 Dune
5 Special 7 Reddish 9 Leant 10 St
11 Inset 17 Anew 18 DD 20 Leas
22 Eat 23 Are

D. ACROSS: 1 Tell 3 Geba 7 Tails 10 Eden
12 Ayes 14 Gum 15 Once 17 Prop
20 Erase 22 Iota 23 Troy
DOWN: 1 True 2 Late 4 Easy 5 Amos
6 Pi 8 Anger 9 Lamps 11 Don 13 Ego
15 Omri 16 Cent 18 Rear 19 Pray 21 Am

E. ACROSS: 1 Solomon 8 Sofas 10 Halt
12 Near 14 Ebo 16 Og 17 Dot 19 Em
21 We 22 No 23 Ornaments 26 An
27 Me 28 It 29 Do
DOWN: 2 Oslo 3 Lot 4 Of 5 Man
6 Oseo 7 The 9 Or 11 Abler
13 Agents 15 Go 17 Dean 18 Them
20 Most 21 Won 24 Nat 25 Ned

17. Regrouping the letters

A.   1. The Lord is my shepherd; I shall not want (Psalm 23: 1)

      2. Blessed art the pure in heart; for they shall see God (Matthew 5: 8)

      3. Follow me, and I will make you fishers of men (Matthew 4: 19)

      4. The wages of sin is death; but the gift of God is eternal life (Romans 6: 23)

      5. Let us run with patience the race that is set before us (Hebrews 12: 1)

      6. Let the peace of God rule in your hearts (Colossians 3: 15)

      7. Bear ye one another's burdens, and so fulfil the law of Christ (Galatians 6: 2)

B.   1. God is our refuge and strength, a very present help in trouble (Psalm 46: 1)

      2. Thy word is a lamp unto my feet, and a light unto my path (Psalm 119: 105)

      3. He that dwelleth in the secret place of the most High shall abide under the shadow of the Almighty (Psalm 91: 1)

      4. A soft answer turneth away wrath (Proverbs 15: 1)

      5. A good name is rather to be chosen than great riches (Proverbs 22: 1)

      6. Remember now thy Creator in the days of thy youth (Ecclesiastes 12: 1)

      7. Prepare ye the way of the Lord, make straight in the desert a highway for our God (Isaiah 40: 3)

18. Crossword

ACROSS: 1 Al   2 Ope   5 On   7 Exile   9 Mar
11 UAR   13 Babylon   16 Erse   17 Edna
18 Attalia   20 Emu   21 Ash   23 Silas   26 Of
27 Fed   28 Or
DOWN: 1 Alm   2 Ox   3 Pity   4 El   6 Nor
7 Erastus   8 Euodias   10 Abram   12 Annas
14 Bet   15 Lel (Ell)   19 Axle   20 Ego   22 Her
24 If   25 Ad

19. A choice of three

A. 1 Ehud   2 Sinai   3 Candace   4 Bethesda
5 Baruch   6 Cyrenius   7 Carpus   8 Elim
9 Gideon   10 Apollos

B. 1 Jubal   2 Laban   3 Ashdod   4 Felix
5 Manoah   6 Azaziah   7 Luz   8 Patmos
9 Simeon   10 Tarsus

C. 1 AD 597   2 John Wesley   3 Holy Land
4 John Newman   5 Epworth
6 Michelangelo   7 Labrador   8 Mary Slessor
9 Joseph of Arimathea   10 Mohammedans

D. 1 Necho   2 Arabia   3 Orpah   4 Narrow
5 Cold   6 Truth   7 Nun   8 Lydia
9 Malchus   10 Lud

E. 1 John Howard   2 Francis of Assisi   3 Lord
Shaftesbury   4 Thomas à Kempis   5 Blood
and Fire   6 William Cowper   7 1674
8 Wilfred Grenfell   9 Henry Martyn
10 Mary Jones

20. Crossword

ACROSS: 1 Cain   2 Day   6 Note   7 Undo
9 Nor   10 Mains   12 Pa   13 And   17 Stain
19 Dodo   21 See   22 Abba   24 Man   25 A lad
DOWN: 1 Chum   2 India   4 Noon   4 Den
5 Yarn   8 Nap   11 Sat   14 Nasal   15 Die
16 Adam   17 Sob   18 Need   20 Dan   23 BA

21. Women of the Bible

1 Miriam   2 Deborah   3 Abigail   4 Elisabeth
5 Jezebel   6 Priscilla   7 Delilah   8 Martha
9 Joanna   10 Herodias

22. Five-letter words

A. 1 Level   2 Leave   3 Endor   4 River
5 Raged   6 Depth   7 Homes   8 Solve
9 Enoch   10 Halve   11 Extol

B. 1 Lydia   2 Anger   3 Rings   4 Speed
5 Ditch   6 Heavy   7 Young   8 Grave
9 Error   10 Regal

C. 1 Hagar   2 Range   3 Eagle   4 Eager
5 Robot   6 Therm   7 Maker   8 Rally
9 Yield   10 Dutch

D. 1 Herod   2 Dream   3 Music   4 Cabin
5 Never   6 Royal   7 Legal   8 Lover
9 Ravel   10 Latch

23. Crossword

ACROSS: 1 Peep 3 Idol 7 Spain 10 Rate
12 Gems 14 Ken 15 Tema 17 Omri 20 Ahira
22 Tell 23 Skye
DOWN: 1 Poor 2 East 4 Dune 5 Loss 6 Ma
8 Pekah 9 Ignor(e) 11 Awe 13 Mar 15 Tent
16 Mail 18 Mark 19 Isle 21 Is

24. Nine lives of a cat

1 Vocation (v. 1) 2 Supplication (v. 9)
3 Communicate (v. 6) 4 Delicate (v. 1) 5 Scattered
(v. 36) 6 Cattle (v. 10) 7 Justification (v. 25)
8 Catch (v. 10) 9 Dedication (v. 22)

25. Mini-crosswords

A. ACROSS: 1 Moses 4 Thine
  DOWN: 1 Mount 2 Sinai 3 Stone
B. ACROSS: 1 Less 4 Ah 5 To 6 True
  DOWN: 1 Light 2 Sat 3 Shone
C. ACROSS: 1 Adore 5 Lo 6 Ur
  7 Capernaum 12 Sat 13 Rag 14 Not
  15 Mow 16 Hid 17 Den 18 Ten 19 Let
  20 Bel
  DOWN: 1 Alp 2 Doer 3 Rung 4 Era
  7 Camel 8 Atone 9 R.A. 10 Unite
  11 Model

26. Hidden people

1 Lot   2 Solomon   3 Abel   4 Herod   5 Hosea
6 Moses   7 Levi   8 Asa   9 Peter   10 Eve

27. Hidden places

1 Lystra   2 Nod   3 Derbe   4 Cana   5 Ur
6 Italy   7 Spain   8 Eden   9 Tyre   10 Gibeon

28. Changing letters

A. W A G E   B. P O O R
   W A R E   P O O L
   W A R T   P O L L
   W A F T   P I L L
   R A F T   P I L E
   R I F T   R I L E
   G I F T   R I C E
                       R I C H

C. S E E D   D. S A N D
   F E E D   S A N K
   F R E D   R A N K
   F R E E   R A C K
   T R E E   R O C K

29. Writing by numbers

A. My grace is sufficient for thee
   (2 Corinthians 12: 9)
B. Trust in the Lord, and do good (Psalm 37: 3)
C. I am the light of the world (John 8: 12)

30. An escape is planned

1 Saul (v. 25) 2 Joab (v. 28) 3 Ishmael (v. 15)
4 David (v. 12) 5 Jotham (v. 21) 6 Jonah
7 Ben-hadad (v. 20)

31. Men in the Gospels

1 Lazarus 2 Caiaphas 3 Barabbas 4 Zebedee
5 Archelaus 6 Alexander 7 Zacharias 8 Cleopas
9 Nathanael 10 Bartholomew

32. Scramble

A. 1 Andrew 2 John 3 Herod 4 Peter
   5 Luke 6 Matthew 7 Judas 8 Paul
B. 1 Adam 2 Abraham 3 Ezra 4 Saul
   5 Joshua 6 Hezekiah 7 Solomon
C. 1 Daniel 2 David 3 Noah 4 Elijah
   5 Moses 6 Eli 7 Jacob 8 Samuel
D. 1 Sarah 2 Mary 3 Dorcas 4 Hagar
   5 Martha 6 Hannah 7 Eve 8 Lydia

33. Crossword

ACROSS: 1 Rob 3 Shoe 6 Ache 7 Pig
8 Emma 10 Up 11 Au 12 Goshen
16 Highroad 19 Aide 20 Bond 21 Run
DOWN: 1 Rope 2 Bag 3 Shepherd 4 Hem
5 Essu 9 Man 10 Us 13 Organ 14 Ahab
15 Eden 17 Hid 18 Oer

34. God's written word

1 Bala 2 India 3 Berea 4 Lamp 5 Ever
6 Sixty-six 7 Onesimus 8 Commandments
9 Inspiration 10 Epistle 11 Twenty-one
12 Youth Initial letters: Bible Society

35. Simon
1 Peter 2 Leper 3 Cyrene 4 Tanner 5 Zelotes
6 Pharisee

36. A ten of 'A's

1 Amminadab 2 Abiathar 3 Aretas 4 Ashan
5 Ananias 6 Ashpenaz 7 Azariah 8 Ahishar
9 Araunah 10 Ahikam

37. Bible insects

1 Grasshopper (v. 5) 2 Locust (v. 25) 3 Moth
(v. 20) 4 Hornet (v. 12) 5 Spider (v. 28) 6 Lice
(v. 17) 7 Worm (v. 7) 8 Gnat (v. 24)
Downwards: Scorpion

38. Paul's travels

A. Neapolis, Mysia, Corinth, Galatia, Ephesus, Cilicia, Athens, Berea
B. Cyprus, Iconium, Antioch, Perga, Paphos, Seleucia, Lystra, Salamis

39. Bible surgery

1 Hyssop (v. 7)   2 Elim (v. 27)   3 Anointed (v. 6)   4 Leper (vv. 2–4)   5 Isaiah (v. 5)   6 Nain (vv. 11–15)   7 Gadarenes (vv. 1,2)   8 Healing (v. 2)

40. At the seaside

1 Anchors (v. 40)   2 Sky (v. 2)   3 Shipwreck (v. 19)   4 Waves (v. 37)   5 Net (v. 6)   6 Fisher (v. 18)   7 Sail (v. 7)   8 Mountains (v. 12)   9 Boat (v. 32)   10 Rocks (v. 29)

41. Making the trio

1 Myrrh   2 John   3 Latin   4 Charity   5 Japheth
6 Stars   7 Peace   8 Walk   9 Glory   10 Withered

42. Building a house

1 Window (v. 28)   2 Roof (v. 4)   3 Door (v. 6)
4 Foundation (v. 48)   5 Brick (v. 7)   6 Upper room (v. 13)

43. Places and people of the Acts

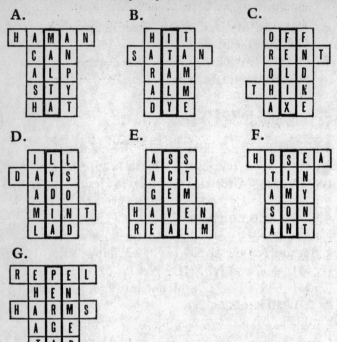

44. Building a text

A. Follow me, and I will make you fishers of men (Matthew 4: 19)

B. I will bless the Lord at all times: his praise shall continually be in my mouth (Psalm 34: 1)

C. Cast thy bread upon the waters: for thou shalt find it after many days (Ecclesiastes 11: 1)

D. Let us run with patience the race that is set before us (Hebrews 12: 1)

E. Eye hath not seen, nor ear heard, neither have entered into the heart of man, the things which God hath prepared for them that love him (1 Corinthians 2: 9)

F. Be not deceived; God is not mocked: for whatsoever a man soweth, that shall he also reap (Galatians 6: 7)

45. Soldier in armour

1 (v. 17) 2 (v. 17) 3 (v. 8) 4 (v. 20) 5 (v. 1)
6 (v. 3) 7 (v. 6)

46. Wives and . . .

1 Handful (v. 12) 2 Understanding (v. 23)
3 Sandals (v. 8) 4 Brand (v. 2) 5 Andrew
6 Notwithstanding (v. 20) 7 Demanded (v. 4)
8 Slander (v. 18)
Initial letters: HUSBANDS

47. God created

1 Eagle 2 Lion 3 Eel 4 Pelican 5 Horse
6 Ass 7 Newt 8 Tiger Across: Elephant

48. All directions

A.

M	W	A	H	B	G	Q	N
W	A	T	E	R	O	V	R
I	Y	H	B	E	F	I	L
P	C	G	F	A	T	N	S
K	L	I	G	D	D	E	U
V	E	L	O	W	X	J	C
Z	A	O	T	R	U	T	H
E	R	Y	B	F	I	D	H

B.

R	N	B	U	F	P	Z	B
G	O	L	D	B	S	C	R
A	R	E	P	P	O	C	A
K	I	E	H	T	G	D	S
Q	D	C	V	E	V	J	S
F	D	A	E	L	A	Y	L
W	O	E	X	T	I	N	M
I	G	N	H	I	J	S	K

C.

S	F	R	B	S	D	P	D
A	Y	H	J	L	N	X	N
F	U	C	E	D	A	R	O
L	I	Y	A	G	K	W	M
C	T	G	A	M	A	F	L
E	V	I	L	O	O	I	A
M	O	A	B	E	C	R	D
Q	P	Z	A	K	V	E	E

49. Baking day
1 Water 2 Salt 3 Egg 4 Bread 5 Milk
6 Mill 7 Oven 8 Oil 9 Flour 10 Crumbs

50. Old Testament prophets

1 Ezekiel 2 Hosea 3 Micah 4 Zephaniah
5 Obadiah 6 Jeremiah 7 Daniel 8 Jonah
9 Nahum   Main column: Zechariah

51. Crossword

ACROSS: 1 Seventh 7 Et 9 Ear 11 Pa
12 Root 14 Iddo 16 Inch 17 Suds 18 Cite
19 Eblt 20 HC 21 Ron 23 El 26 Stanley
DOWN: 2 Ex 3 Era 4 To 5 Jericho 6 Close
follower of Jesus 8 Tonic. 9 Ether 10 Risen
11 Addle 13 Oct 15 Dub 22 Own 24 St
25 Me